Hiawyn Oram

Sarah Warburton

the Rumblewick Letters

My Unwilling Witch

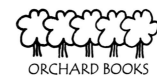

ORCHARD BOOKS

This is Rumblewick Spellwacker Mortimer B (RB for short). He is a Witch's Familiar, or extra qualified witch's cat.

WITCH'S FAMILIAR LICENCE

1. B
2. RUMBLEWICK SPELLWACKER MORTIMER
3. HEYDAY 16th WIZTON-UNDER-WOLD
BRSM7552623J9YR 13

WFL

WFL LICENCING OFFICE

This is Haggy Aggy. For the next seven years, she is his WITCH and he is her CAT.

(Check out his contract at the back of this book!)

Rumblewick's job is to take care of Haggy Aggy and help her be a **PROPER** witch at all times.

RB's Uncle Sherbet – a retired Witch's Familiar – with his wife, Aunt Figgy

But this is not easy, as these letters to his Uncle Sherbet show.

Haggy Aggy **DOES NOT** want to be a proper witch. She wants to be anything **BUT** a witch. She wants to be . . .

. . . READ ON AND SEE!

Thirteen Chimneys
Wizton-under-Wold
Fogsday the 15th

Dear Uncle Sherbet,

You always said that if I was in trouble, I should turn to you for help. Now I am. HELP! It looks like my witch doesn't want to be a witch. She refuses to cackle. She won't get on a broomstick if she can help it. She's banned frogs' legs, newts' eyes, bat wings etc from our potions. AND she's completely turned against frightening children. All she wants to do is shop, watch telly and make some friends who aren't witches.

What shall I do?

Your nephew,

Rumblewick Spellwacker Mortimer B.

PS: Her name is Haggy Aggy (HA for short).

Read this — U.S. x

Rumblewick
13 Chimneys
Wizton Under Wold

MOULDY OLD COTTAGE
FLYING TEAPOT STREET
PRANCETOWN

Wartsun

My Dear Rumblewick,

I'm sorry to hear about your problem. In all my years as a Witch's Familiar, I never heard of a witch who didn't want to be one. Even so, I've dusted down my old 'Book of Spells' and found something that may be of use. Here it is. Let me know how you get on!

Your loving,

Uncle Sherbet

Cauldron Inks LTD
midnight black

Thirteen Chimneys
Wizton-under-Wold

Oldenday the 26th

Dear Uncle Sherbet,

Thank you for your letter and Spell. But . . .

BAD NEWS! While I was out collecting the slime for it, HA slipped off to the video store. On the way, she met a crocodile of children. She followed them to the library for Story Time, and turned herself into a **pot plant** so she could listen without **scaring** them.

And here's the **worst** bit. The stories were all about beautiful princesses marrying handsome princes. Now she's ordered me to write a letter to our local palace **demanding** the prince comes to meet her. I NEVER disobey my witch. For her own sake, is this one time when I should?

Please advise urgently.

RB.

Squish!!!

Found this !!

oh dear . . . .

OOPS! ←

Ha Ha!

Thirteen Chimneys
Washday the 14th

Dear Uncle,

It's getting <u>WORSE</u>. HA has bought a glittering ballgown, dance slippers and a tiara. Now she's teetering around with spell books on her head trying to walk like a beautiful princess! Also, she made me write that letter to the prince and cover it with s̲t̲i̲c̲k̲e̲r̲s̲. The thing is, it's ALL lies. She isn't a princess, she's a <u>WITCH</u>. And I think the prince will notice. What now?

RB.

PS: She's told me to turn a cauliflower into a glass coach to meet her prince in. I've searched EVERYWHERE for a spell, but can't find one.

Can you help?

Spilled coffee, sorry!

Mad!

2nd

Help!

This is a copy of the letter HA made me write to the prince →

Somewhere
I Bet You Wish
You Knew Where
Washday the 14th

HA
4
P

Dear Your PRINCE,

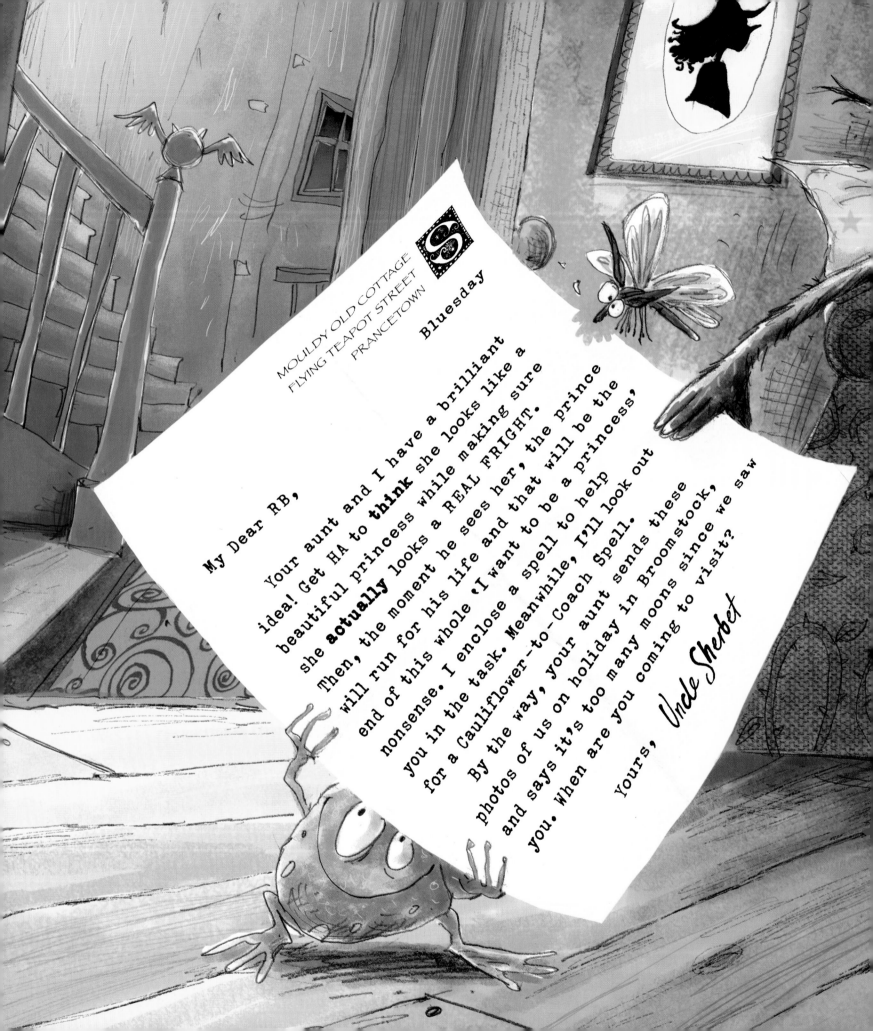

MOULDY OLD COTTAGE
FLYING TEAPOT STREET
PRANCETOWN

Bluesday

My Dear RB,

Your aunt and I have a brilliant idea! Get HA to **think** she looks like a beautiful princess while making sure she **actually** looks a REAL FRIGHT. Then, the moment he sees her, the prince will run for his life and that will be the end of this whole 'I want to be a princess' nonsense. I enclose a spell to help you in the task. Meanwhile, I'll look out for a Cauliflower-to-Coach Spell.

By the way, your aunt sends these photos of us on holiday in Broomstock, and says it's too many moons since we saw you. When are you coming to visit?

Yours, Uncle Sherbet

If undelivered return to:

MOULDY OLD COTTAGE
FLYING TEAPOT STREET
PRANCETOWN

tadpole

Failed attempt!

Thirteen Chimneys

Day of the Night of the Prince Thing

Dear Uncle Sherbet,

Your uglifying idea is brilliant, thank you! I've learned the spell and found a pond full of (frothing) frog spawn.

By the way, don't worry about the Cauliflower-to-Coach Spell. My best friend, Grimey, found one. (He's cat to Witch Understairs next door.) OK, so his spell turned the cauli into a rocking horse, but I've told HA that's what the BEST princesses are using to meet princes on.

So far she believes me.

Think of me tonight. xxx RB.

...rbet
Old Cottage
Flying Teapot Street
PRANCETOWN

1ST

Another
failed attempt
(ha ha!)

WITCH
OF THE
YEAR
Awarded to
WITCH UNDERSTAIRS

Grimey!!

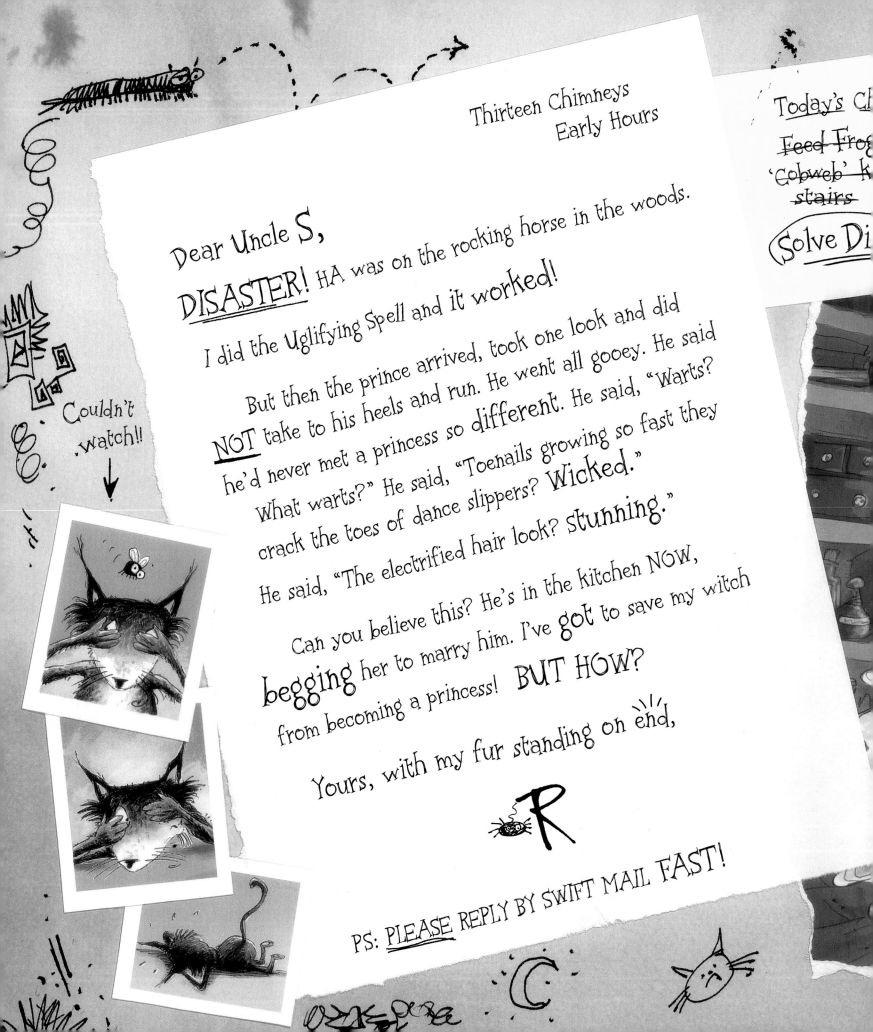

Thirteen Chimneys
Early Hours

Dear Uncle S,

DISASTER! HA was on the rocking horse in the woods.

I did the Uglifying Spell and it worked!

But then the prince arrived, took one look and did NOT take to his heels and run. He went all gooey. He said he'd never met a princess so different. He said, "Warts? What warts?" He said, "Toenails growing so fast they crack the toes of dance slippers? Wicked."

He said, "The electrified hair look? Stunning."

Can you believe this? He's in the kitchen NOW, begging her to marry him. I've got to save my witch from becoming a princess! BUT HOW?

Yours, with my fur standing on end,

R

PS: PLEASE REPLY BY SWIFT MAIL FAST!

Couldn't watch!!

Today's Ch
~~Feed Frog~~
'Cobweb' k
~~stairs~~
Solve Di

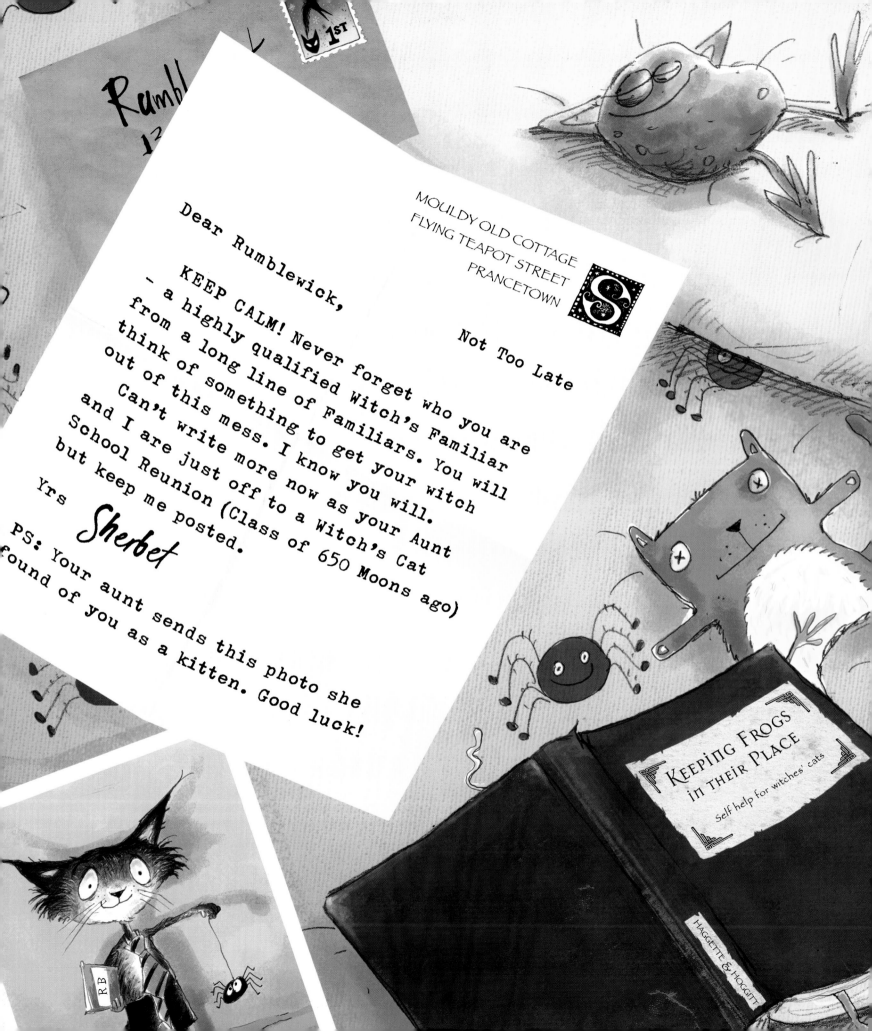

MOULDY OLD COTTAGE
FLYING TEAPOT STREET
PRANCETOWN

Not Too Late

Dear Rumblewick,

KEEP CALM! Never forget who you are – a highly qualified Witch's Familiar from a long line of Familiars. You will think of something to get your witch out of this mess. I know you will.

Can't write more now as your Aunt and I are just off to a Witch's Cat School Reunion (Class of 650 Moons ago) but keep me posted.

Yrs

Sherbet

PS: Your aunt sends this photo she found of you as a kitten. Good luck!

KEEPING FROGS in their PLACE

self help for witches' cats

HAGGETTE & HOGGITT

Pea juice →

Wytch!

Thirteen Chimneys
Sunshineyday, the 12th this year

Dear Uncle Sherbet,

Well, I don't know quite HOW but things have worked out! HA asked the prince to go and slay the Under-Wytch-Wood DRAGON that keeps her awake at night snoring and he started trembling like a jelly! This made her suspect that he wasn't a real prince. So she told me to pile up 10 mattresses with a pea on the bottom layer. She said, like in the fairy story, if he WAS really royal, he'd feel the pea through anything. Well, as I was piling, I had my idea. I wouldn't put a pea anywhere. Who'd know?

P.T.O

① 1

Princess & the PEA

↑ mushy pea!

Grrrrr!

Prince ha ha

Ye Olde Beast of Wytch Wood

And no one did. The prince lay down. HA asked him if he was OK or if he could feel a pea sticking into him . . . He said no (of course he did, there was no pea). She declared him a <u>fake</u>, turned him into a walking pumpkin and told him to scarper. I don't know which makes me happier – that she's **not** marrying a prince or that she's performed a **decent** spell for the FIRST time in moons!

By the way, she's giving me two spring days off next Hayfever Month. Maybe I can visit then? With loads of thanks for all your help – and to Aunt Figgy.

Your loving nephew,

Rumblewick Spellwacker Mortimer B.

PS: The UGLIFYING SPELL wears off overnight and HA is looking back to **normal!**

PPS: Mind you, better not count my tadpoles before they hatch, right now she's watching The Nutcracker Ballet on TV. Next thing she'll want to become a ballerina!?!

If undelivered return to:

13 CHIMNEYS
WIZTON-UNDER-WOLD

Here's a copy →
of the Pumpkin Spell

CONTRACT OF SERVICE

between

WITCH HAGATHA AGATHA, Haggy Aggy for short, HA for shortest

of Thirteen Chimneys, Wizton-under-Wold

&

the Witch's Familiar,

Rumblewick Spellwacker Mortimer B, RB for short

It is hereby agreed that, come

FIRE, Brimstone, CAULDRONS overflowing

or ALIEN WIZARDS invading,

for the NEXT 7 YEARS

RB will serve HA,

obey her EVERY WHIM AND WORD and at all times assist her

in the ways of being a true and proper WITCH.

PAYMENT for services will be:

* a log basket to sleep in   *   unlimited Slime Buns for breakfast

* free use of HA's broomsticks (outside of peak brooming hours)

and a cracked mirror for luck.

PENALTY for failing in his duties will be decided on the whim of

THE HAGS ON HIGH.

SIGNED AND SEALED

this New Moon Day, 22nd of Remember

Haggy Aggy
....
Witch Hagatha Agatha

Rumblewick
....
Rumblewick Spellwacker Mortimer B

Trixie Fiddlestick
....
And witnessed by the High Hag, Trixie Fiddlestick

ORCHARD BOOKS

338 Euston Road, London NW1 3BH
Orchard Books Australia
Hachette Children's Books
Level 17/207 Kent Street, Sydney NSW 2000

ISBN-10: 1 84616 063 4
ISBN-13: 978 1 84616 063 9

First published in 2006 by Orchard Books

A CIP catalogue record for this book is
available from the British Library.

Orchard Books is a division
of Hachette Children's Books

1 3 5 7 9 10 8 6 4 2
Printed in China

Magic

who grow books on trees at

Who are these people?

I wrote these letters!

??

!?

No more shopping, PLEASE !!!

Watch out for potplants with boots and pointy noses!

Grimey's House

13 Chimneys

Me

Oops!

Frog Pen!